Using Markdown

A Short Instruction Guide

by

William Dyer

Using Markdown: A Short Instruction Guide

William Dyer

Copyright © 2018. William Dyer.

Table of Contents

Introduction

I discovered Markdown while I was in search of a method to simplify the process of preserving documents. Markdown certainly makes text repairs easier, and I was pleasantly surprised at how much it made all of my other writing tasks easier as well. Today, I perform every writing task with Markdown.

When we create a Markdown document, we write text, adding only a few extra keyboard characters to create emphasis, lists, insert images and more--all without making the document hard to read. Markdown focuses on what is important: creating content, not on presentation. We can write, using only a small set of syntax rules, while Markdown does the conversion. If you use text for your drafts, it can take you a long way in simplifying the work. Even the draft can look good--and Markdown converts it to HTML for us.

Markdown's format for writing has become quite popular. Today, we see it used as a part of a web site's editing features. There are Markdown plug-ins on blogging sites setting the writer to free to write instead of concerning themselves with formatting. As a Web writing tool, Markdown is excellent. That Markdown is used in GitHub, GitBook, Reddit, Stack Overflow, and many others, is proof of this. Authors can use Markdown to write articles and books. While John Gruber's basic Markdown may not be sufficient for creating books, extensions such as CommonMark, MultiMarkdown, Pandoc, etc. can take up that slack.

This book is introductory and covers John Gruber's basic Markdown. Information on extensions, which add more features to Markdown, is readily available if you need it, but knowing how to use basic Markdown will carry over into the use of those extensions--John Gruber's Markdown is the standard. Here, then, we'll cover basic Markdown syntax with examples to show you how you can use it right away. I think that you will be pleasantly surprised at just how much basic Markdown can do.

I have avoided including instructions on how to install Markdown. Most Markdown editors use a common installation program, so the installation of a Markdown editor is no different than most other programs. Also, most Markdown editors today have Markdown features built in, so if you have a Markdown editor installed, chances are superb that the editor will have the ability to at least export your content to HTML. With a good Markdown editor, a beginner can get started with their writing right away.

If you aren't a Markdown user, and you work with a good amount of text, you may decide to give it a try. If you're already a user, and this book gives you ideas on how to be more productive, so much the better. Lastly, if you read this book and decide that Markdown isn't for you, that's good too. Sometimes, a change in an already productive routine is not beneficial and if this book shows you that, then it will have served that purpose as well--but I hope you enjoy the book.

What is Markdown?

Credit for Markdown goes to John Gruber and Aaron Swartz--Gruber as the creator and Swartz as the sole beta tester and contributor. Markdown was created as a simple way for non-programmers to write in; it is a text tool that allows anyone to create Web pages without knowing any HTML. Here's a direct quote from John Gruber's Markdown project page:

> Markdown is a text-to-HTML conversion tool for web writers. Markdown allows you to write using an easy-to-read, easy-to-write plain text format, then convert it to structurally valid XHTML (or HTML).

Formatting is done using plain text symbols and punctuation marks. A perl script, that runs in the background, converts the text into HTML. Markdown's aim was to make writing as easy to create, and as readable, as possible.

The main source of inspiration for Markdown's syntax is the format of straight text email. In the early days of email, formatting text wasn't possible; it was all plain text. Back then, just as it is today, all caps was frowned upon so users came up with the convention of using various punctuation marks to indicate a style of some sort to make a word or phrase stand out. Today, email is far more advanced with formatting features, so we rarely use characters in formatting, but Markdown sticks to that old tradition.

Markdown addresses issues that can be expressed in plain text. It was designed as a format for *writing* for the web, but it is not a replacement for HTML. Markdown makes it easier to read, write, and edit prose--it is a *writing* format. HTML is a *publishing* format.

Choosing a Text Editor

To write Markdown text, at a bare minimum, you need a plain text editor. A text editor is a program that lets you edit plain text. Text editors are normally provided with operating systems and software development packages, so you probably have one preinstalled on your system already. Notepad, for example, on Windows machines, is a text editor. Text editors can be used to change configuration files, documentation, and program source code.

There is a type of plain text editor that is geared specifically to working with Markdown. These editors have added functionality in that you can see what your Markdown documents look like in HTML as you write. Such editors are called Markdown editors. Markdown formatted text is easy to read as it is, so the added feature of seeing formatted HTML output isn't completely necessary, but it can be quite handy.

Markdown was designed to export text to HTML. As Markdown editors are essentially plain text editors, they save files as plain text, but an option to export the file as an HTML file is present. Depending on the editor, there may also be an option to export the text as PDF.

Because I work on different machines and operating systems, I have collected what I think, is a set of tools that works well for me. Some might think it a rather odd setup, but on the other hand, some would say that we can never have too many tools. Here is a short list of the programs that I use. Perhaps you will find one or two of them useful.

When I work on Windows or Linux systems, I prefer Ghostwriter, which can be found at:

https://wereturtle.github.io/ghostwriter/

Ghostwriter was the first Markdown editor I have used and, having used it for so long, I have grown rather partial to it. Ghostwriter was built with the writer in mind and it has features to that end.

Ghostwriter opens files in separate windows. This works well for me when I have research data in one file, a beginning draft of a paper in another file, and so on. I also like to use it in the editing phase of a written project for the same reasons in that I can still keep research data (so I can double-check the information) separate from the draft.

Occasionally, I do have to play the part of a programmer, and in such cases, I choose between one of these editors:

Sublime
http://www.sublimetext.com/

Atom
https://atom.io/

These editors have Markdown plug-ins that extend their usefulness. This allows me to write code and documentation within the same environment. Each of these editors are available for Windows, Linux, and Mac systems.

Editors such as Sublime and Atom, have features useful to programmers, so they may be a bit complex for some writers. There are two notable Markdown-only editors available for Windows, Mac, and Linux machines. If having the same editor on multiple systems is important to you, give these excellent editors a try:

Typora
https://typora.io/

Caret
https://caret.io/

There are times when I want to use a Markdown editor that has a unique feature or is just nice to use. I may not use them often, but I think that they are worth keeping around. Here are three that I launch on occasion:

Windows: MarkdownPad 2 Pro
http://www.Markdownpad.com/

Linux: ReText
https://github.com/retext-project/retext/

Mac: iA Writer
https://ia.net/writer/support/mac/

I mention these three because I like how they can open multiple documents in a single window. I can access them through tabs or a menu, handy for working on multiple chapters or sections of a paper (I like to keep chapters or sections in separate files, joining them together, later in the project). While the preview window can also be displayed, it's in the same window as well, taking away some of the writing area, but I can turn that off or on at will.

There are many other Markup editors that you can try. Each Markdown editor has a certain feature that is different from the others. I use other editors as well, depending on the tasks I have to perform. The ones I've mentioned here do well for me and are more than sufficient in most work.

It is important to use a plain text editor when writing Markdown, so it is best to avoid word processors. Word processors, such as Microsoft Word, WordPad, OpenOffice, LibreOffice, and so on, are not plain text editors. Formatting and styling are performed by the use of invisible, non-text characters (called metadata) which can cause problems with text and HTML files. Word processors have their place, but Markdown and HTML both require plain text.

Headings

Headings are those lines that we use for section titles, such as chapter titles and topic / sub-topic titles. With Markdown, we can use two types of heading types: *setext* and *atx*.

Setext-style headings are underlined. When we use underlining to create headings, we are limited to two: equal signs are used for first-level (H1) headings and dashes are used for second-level (H2) headings. For example, here are two titles of articles I found during research on the 19th century American West some time ago. The first uses first-level styling and the second uses the second-level styling:

```
HOW TO REPEL TRAIN ROBBERS.
============================

BRIGANDAGE ON OUR RAILROADS.
----------------------------
```

You can use any number of ='s or -'s that you wish, for this to work. As you can see in the above example, I underlined the entire titles, but you can use only one = and - if you want. This is what the output looks like:

HOW TO REPEL TRAIN ROBBERS.

BRIGANDAGE ON OUR RAILROADS.

Incidentally, periods are no longer used at the end of titles, but during the time these pieces were written, ending a title with a period was common practice. I opted to keep the period in place, in these examples.

With atx-style headings, we have a greater range; we can use up to six heading levels. Between underlining and using hash tags, I prefer the latter. All we need to do is place one to six hash characters at the start of the line, corresponding to heading levels 1-6: the number of opening hashes determines the heading level. For example:

```
# H1
## H2
### H3
#### H4
##### H5
###### H6
```

Markdown will give us the following:

H1

H2

H3

H4

H5

H6

Be aware that not all Markdown editors require a
space between the hash tags and the title while other
editors do require it. Markdown requires the space.
If you find that your editor doesn't require the
space, consider adding it anyway. There might be
an occasion when you have to use a different editor
that follows Markdown's rule and if your
Markdown document doesn't have the space
between the hash marks and the title text, your
headings will not render properly.

We can "close" atx-style headings by adding hash
marks to the end of the line, but this is a cosmetic
option; it isn't necessary. I don't use closing hash
marks, but if you think it looks better, by all means,
add them.

Whether you use closing hash marks or not, will not
affect the document. In fact, if you do decide to use
closing hash marks, the closing hash marks do not
even need to match the number of hashes used to
open the heading (remember: only the number of
opening hashes determines the heading level). For
example, if we type:

```
# H1 #
## H2 ##
### H3 ######
```

15

Lastly, you are not limited to one style or another; you can use underlining and hashes. For example, you might want to use setext-style underlining for H1 and H2, and use atx-style for the headings, H3-H6.

Emphasis

The general technique of showing emphasis, in Western typography, is through a change or modification of font such as: italic type, bold type, small caps, changing letter case, s p a c i n g, underlining, color, and *additional graphic marks*. In this section, we'll concern ourselves only with italic and bold type.

Italic type was first used in 1500. Initially, it was used in small, pocket-sized books to replicate handwritten manuscripts common at the time. The use of italic type as emphasis began in the sixteenth century and was the accepted norm by the early seventeenth. Bold type is a more recent invention, appearing in the nineteenth century.

In Markdown, we use asterisks * or underscores _ to show emphasis:

```
*single asterisks* will italicize text
_single underscores_ will italicize text
**double asterisks** will bold text
__double underscores__ will bold text
```

will produce:

> *single asterisks* will italicize text
> *single underscores* will italicize text
> **double asterisks** will bold text
> **double underscores** will bold text

You can use either character, but you have to use the same character to surround the text. There is no mix-n-match here; you can't use an asterisk on one side of the text and an underscore on the other. Choose and use either asterisks or underscores around the word or phrase that you want to emphasize.

Emphasis can be used in the middle of a word. For example, in crime shows, when a person is asked whether or not they committed the crime, the guilty one seems to always answer:

Ab-**SO-lute**-ly not!

There are no spaces between the asterisk or the underscore in emphasized text. If you surround an * or _ with spaces, it'll be treated as an asterisk or underscore character.

Sometimes, we might want to show emphasis by showing a formatting character. For example, we might want to show asterisks at the beginning and end of a line of text. To prevent Markdown from using the asterisk as a formatting character, we `escape` it. Escaping is a method to use something outside of its intended function.

To produce a literal asterisk or underscore at a position where it would otherwise be used as an emphasis mark, you can escape it by adding a backslash:

```
**Shop and save at our store!!!**
\*We cheat the other guy and pass the
savings on to you!\*
```

We will see:

Shop and save at our store!
We cheat the other guy and pass the savings on to you!

Paragraphs and Line Breaks

A paragraph is a collection of related sentences to cover a single topic. In turn, paragraphs support and connect to one another making up a complete written work, such as a short story, essay, academic research paper, a book, and so on. Paragraphs help organize writing, combining similar ideas together and developing key ideas that the work intends to present.

How a coherent and understandable paragraph is created is beyond the scope of this book; a good writing book can help with that, but Markdown has its rules of formatting that you should know: A paragraph is a block of text and should not be indented with spaces or tabs. It can have one line or many lines. A paragraph break is made by hitting the `<Enter>` key twice; paragraphs are separated by a blank line.

This description may seem overly simplified, but Markdown is strict about it. Markdown does not support "hard-wrapped" text paragraphs. That is, hitting the `<Enter>` key once will not force text to a new line in the final output. Yet, there will be times when we may need to break up paragraphs with some way to break up a line. Poetry comes to mind.

Markdown does have a way to do this: a line break is made by ending a line with *two or more spaces* and then hit the `<Enter>` key once.

We can't see the ending spaces in a book, so the following example will be surrounded with quotes, just to show the limits of the line and the ending spaces:

```
"This line has two spaces at the end.   "
```

To see that this can be done, let's try a small example. The following little ditty will have four lines. Again, although we can't see them in this book, the first three lines ends with two spaces at the end of the line, while the fourth line will end with two taps of the `<Enter>` key to ensure that a blank line ends the paragraph. This is what our output will look like:

This computer is a stupid thing,
I think that we should sell it.
It never does what I want it to,
but only what I tell it.

Adding two spaces at the end of a line, to create a line break, can be a pain to get used to at first. This is a little more effort--adding two spaces at the end of each line rather than hitting `<Enter>` once--but I agree with John Gruber, the creator of Markdown, here. The view of every line break is equivalent to hitting the `<Enter>` once (or the HTML equivalent, `<br />`) rule doesn't work for Markdown.

Markdown's email-style blockquoting and multi-paragraph list items work best using hard breaks. It looks better too.

Again, a paragraph break is made by hitting the `<Enter>` key twice and a line break is made by adding two spaces to the end of the line and hitting the `<Enter>` key once. If you were to forget to add the two spaces, and hit the `<Enter>` key once, you would see the line we thought would be separated, strung together as part of a standard paragraph.

We might wonder then, if adding two spaces will force a new line? What about folks who add two spaces at the end of a sentence? We certainly wouldn't want our paragraphs broken into single lines, so let's see what happens. If we type:

```
Two spaces are after the period.  Did this
new sentence become a new line?
```

we get the following result:

> Two spaces are after the period. Did this new sentence become a new line?

We see that the paragraph remains intact; we can still use two spaces after a period, or any other punctuation mark, that ends a sentence. It is only when we use two spaces *and* the `<Enter>` key that we create a line break.

Blockquotes

Markdown uses the email-style > character for blockquotes. If you're familiar with quoting passages of text in an email message, then you know how to create a blockquote in Markdown. Some people recommend that each line begin with a > character. It looks structured and can better show the organization of the document. If you decide to use this method, you will have to hard wrap (press the `<Enter>` key at the end of each line) the text and put a > before every line:

```
> This is a blockquote with two paragraphs.
This is
> paragraph one. Some quotes we'll encounter
are large,
> true, but I sometimes wonder if these are
used by some
> students to act as filler material in
their papers.

> And this is paragraph two. It is only one
sentence long,
> but with the inclusion of this one, I
guess it is
> two sentences now.
```

For those of us who would rather type as few characters as possible, Markdown will not complain if you only put the > before the first line of a paragraph:

```
> This is a blockquote with two paragraphs.
This is paragraph one. Some quotes we'll
encounter are large, true, but I sometimes
```

```
wonder if these are used by some students to
act as filler material in their papers.

> And this is paragraph two. It is only one
sentence long, but with the inclusion of
this one, I guess it is two sentences now.
```

Either method will give us the following output:

> This is a blockquote with two paragraphs. This is
> paragraph one. Some quotes we'll encounter are large,
> true, but I sometimes wonder if these are used by some
> students to act as filler material in their papers.
>
> And this is paragraph two. It is only one sentence long,
> but with the inclusion of this one, I guess it is two
> sentences now.

Blockquotes can contain other Markdown elements,
including headers, emphasis, lists, and code blocks:

```
> ### This is a H3 header.

> 1. This is item1.
> 2. This is item2.

> This is a line of text:

> and the following is a code block.

>       #include <stdio.h>
>       int main()
>       {
>           printf("Hello, World!");
>           return 0;
>       }
```

Blockquotes can be nested (a blockquote-within-a-
blockquote) by adding additional > characters. Here

is a sample from a restoration of Elizabeth Carter's translation of Epictetus' *Enchiridion*. This is pericope 52, which ends the book. It lends itself well to be a nested blockquote example as well as a chance to add a few embellishments:

> **52**. Upon all occasions we ought to
> have these maxims ready at hand:

>> "Conduct me, Jove, and you, O Destiny,
>> Wherever your decrees have fixed my
>> station."
>> *Cleanthes*

>> "I follow cheerfully; and, did I not,
>> Wicked and wretched, I must follow still
>> Whoever yields properly to Fate, is
>> deemed
>> Wise among men, and knows the laws of
>> heaven."
>> *Euripides, Frag. 965*

> And this third:

>> "O Crito, if it thus pleases the gods,
>> thus let it be. Anytus and Melitus may kill
>> me indeed, but hurt me they cannot."
>> *Plato's Crito and Apology*

Code Blocks

Pre-formatted code blocks are used for writing about programming or markup source code, such as HTML. In my line of work, I have to show and explain code often, so I make heavy use of this feature as well as code spans. Rather than forming normal paragraphs, the lines of a code block are interpreted literally. They are also styled with a different font so it is easier to see the difference between code and normal text.

To create a code block in Markdown, indent every line of the block by at least 4 spaces or 1 tab. For example:

```
This is a code block.
```

Here is another example:

```
#include <stdio.h>
int main()
{
    // printf() displays the string inside
quotation
    printf("Hello, World!");
    return 0;
}
```

A code block can range from one line to many (this range is called a block). A code block continues until it reaches a line that is not indented (or the end of the article).

When you create a code block, ampersands & and angle brackets < and > are treated as literal characters. This makes it very easy to include example HTML source code using Markdown--just copy-n-paste it the code, indent it, and Markdown will handle the rest.

Regular Markdown syntax is not processed within code blocks. Asterisks, for example, are actual asterisk characters within a code block--not as a formatting character.

You aren't limited to just using code this way; you can do this with regular text. For example:

```
Sometimes I carry classic books
just so others will think that
I am intelligent.
```

This is handy for those times when you do not want to do any extra formatting of the text outside of displaying it as-is.

Code Spans

A code span indicates code within a normal paragraph. For example:

```
In a C program, use the `printf()` function
to display information.
```

will show:

> In a C program, use the `printf()` function to display
> information.

To include a literal backtick character, also called
an *accent grave*, within a code span, you can use
multiple backticks as the opening and closing
delimiters:

```
``There is a literal backtick ` here.``
```

which will produce this:

> There is a literal backtick ` here.

The backtick delimiters surrounding a code span
may include spaces--one after the opening and one
before the closing. This allows you to place literal
backtick characters at the beginning or end of a
code span:

```
A single backtick in a code span: `` ` ``

A backtick-delimited string in a code
span: `` `bar` ``
```

will produce:

> A single backtick in a code span: `` ` ``
>
> A backtick-delimited string in a code span: `` `bar` ``

With a code span, ampersands and angle brackets are encoded as HTML entities automatically, which makes it easy to include example HTML tags. Markdown will turn this:

```
The beginning of a paragraph in HTML starts
with a `<p>` tag and the end of the
paragraph is closed with a `</p>` tag.
```

into:

> The beginning of a paragraph in HTML starts with a <p> tag and the end of the paragraph is closed with a </p> tag.

You can write this:

```
`&amp;` is the way to code an ampersand `&`
in HTML.
```

to produce:

> & is the way to code an ampersand & in HTML.

Lists

Lists have been around for as long as there has been writing. Lists of laws, for example, date back as far as 2100 BCE. Earlier codes are known to have existed, but the *Code of Ur-Nammu*, written around 2100 BCE, is the earliest legal text in existence, predating the *Code of Hammurabi* by 300 years. Lists, it seems, have always been a big deal.

Lists help readers understand, remember, and review key points; follow a sequence of actions or events; and break up long stretches of straight text. They are useful as they emphasize selected blocks of information in the main text. When you see a group of three or four items grouped as a list on a page, rather than in normal paragraph format, we tend to see it as a sign to pay close attention.

Lists can have several uses, For example, in instructions, they can be used to spell out individual steps in a process. Lists can add an aesthetic quality; adding a bit of visual variety in that they spread out the material, creating more white space.

Markdown supports unordered (bullet) and ordered (numbered) lists.

Unordered Lists

Unordered lists use asterisks, the plus symbol, and hyphen--and they can be used interchangeably.

```
* Red
* White
* Blue
```

is equivalent to:

```
+ Red
+ White
+ Blue
```

and:

```
- Red
- White
- Blue
```

And if you want to mix-n-match:

```
* Red
- White
+ Blue
```

No matter which arrangement we choose, this will be our output:

- Red
- White
- Blue

List markers typically start at the left margin, but may be indented by up to three spaces. List markers must be followed by one or more spaces or a tab.

List items may consist of multiple paragraphs. Each subsequent paragraph in a list item must be indented by either 4 spaces or one tab:

```
* NASA's Apollo Rockets and Spacecraft:

   The flight mode, lunar orbit rendezvous,
was selected in 1962. The boosters were the
Saturn IB for Earth orbit flights and the
Saturn V for lunar flights.

   Apollo was a three-part spacecraft: the
command module (CM), the crew's quarters,
and flight control section; the service
module (SM) for the propulsion and
spacecraft support systems (when together,
the two modules are called CSM); and the
lunar module (LM), to take two of the crew
to the lunar surface, support them on the
Moon, and return them to the CSM in lunar
orbit.

* While we tend to remember only manned
Apollo missions, there were several unmanned
Apollo-Saturn missions as well.
```

You can indent each line of a paragraph if you think the alignment looks better, or you can allow the paragraphs to wrap naturally, as I have in the above example. Markdown allows either preference.

As we can with paragraphs, blockquotes can also be inserted into a list. To do this, the blockquote > delimiter needs to be indented:

```
* A list item with a blockquote:

    > This is a blockquote inside a list
item.
```

To put a code block within a list item, the code block needs to be indented twice--8 spaces or two tabs:

```
* A list item with a code block:

    <!DOCTYPE html>
    <html>
    <body>
    <h1>This is a heading</h1>
    <p>This is a paragraph.</p>
    </body>
    </html>
```

Ordered Lists

Ordered lists use numbers followed by a period:

```
1. skateboard
2. scooter
3. bicycle
```

Our example, above, shows the list starting at 1, but Markdown doesn't care what number you start with and how you number the list. The output will always begin with 1, the next item as 2, the next as 3, and so on.

You can create your numbered list using all 1s, like this:

```
1. skateboard
1. scooter
1. bicycle
```

or use any random number:

```
7. skateboard
4. scooter
9. bicycle
```

The output would still be the same. To prove the point, let's see the output of the latest example of the list, numbered, 7, 4, and 9:

1. skateboard
2. scooter
3. bicycle

You can be orderly in how you number your lists, but you don't have to.

A word of caution here: John Gruber, the creator of Markdown, warns that, if you do use odd list numbering, you should still start the list with the number 1. At some point in the future, Markdown may support starting ordered lists at an arbitrary number. I am not sure if this has been formally implemented yet, but some Markdown editors already support this and will accept odd numbering.

Nested Lists

So far, our lists have been rather simple, but it is possible to add more detail to our lists with sublist items. To create nested (sublist) items in our list, we just indent those items by pressing the `<Tab>` key, or by at least four spaces:

Nested Unordered List

```
* Tree
  - partridge
  - pear
* turtle doves
* french hens
```

We can do the same with numbered lists. If we type out the following:

```
1. Tree
   1. partridge
   2. pear
2. turtle doves
3. french hens
```

With nesting, we can create more complex lists to include using unordered items as well as numbered items. Remember that you can still embellish text, insert paragraphs, blockquotes, and code blocks as well. Here is a more detailed example of what we can do with the NASA example, above:

```
1. NASA's Apollo Rockets and Spacecraft

   The flight mode, lunar orbit rendezvous,
was selected in 1962. The boosters were:
```

```
   * the Saturn IB for Earth orbit flights
   * the Saturn V for lunar flights.

   Apollo was a three-part spacecraft:

   1. the command module (CM), the crew's
quarters and flight control section
   2. the service module (SM) for propulsion
and spacecraft support systems
   3. (when SM combined with CM, the two
modules are called CSM)
   4. the lunar module (LM)

      1. took two crewmen to the lunar
surface
      2. provided for their support on the
Moon
      3. returned them to the CSM.

2. Missions

   1. manned Apollo missions
   2. unmanned Apollo-Saturn missions
```

One more caveat: Before closing our discussion of lists, John Gruber points out one more issue. If you start a sentence with a number, it is possible to trigger an ordered list by accident. In other words, a *number-period-space* sequence at the beginning of a line of text is what triggers a list. To avoid this, backslash-escape the period and the line of text will work correctly:

```
1866\. First known U.S. train robbery. Oct
6; Reno Gang.
```

Links

As we write our documents, whether it be a paper, blog, or Web pages, there will probably be an opportunity to refer to other information. Quoting can help, but it may not be enough. Through the use of links, sometimes called "hyperlinks," we can access external data.

The first widely used open Internet protocol (that included hyperlinks from any Internet site to any other Internet site) was the Gopher protocol, released in 1991. It was soon replaced by HTML upon the appearance of the Mosaic browser in 1993. Not only could it handle Gopher links, it handled HTML links as well. HTML had the greater advantage of being able to mix graphics, text, and hyperlinks, whereas Gopher was more limited, only handling menu-structured text and hyperlinks.

Links are references to other content as well as the method to get to it. Click on a link to a different document, and we can see it. Since Markdown was designed to create Web pages, it has link support.

Basic Markdown only supports linking to outside documents; it doesn't like internal anchors (linking within the same document), but it can be done by adding some HTML. Here, we will cover the linking that basic Markdown does support.

Automatic Links

The easiest way to create a link in Markdown is to create what is called an *automatic link*. Markdown supports this shortcut style on URLs and email addresses. To accomplish this, all that we need to do is to surround the URL or email address with angle brackets. What this means is that if you want to show the actual text of a URL or email address, and also have it be a clickable link. If you want to link to John Gruber's Markdown page (he is the creator of Markdown), you can type this:

```
<https://daringfireball.net/projects/Markdown/>
```

The text within the angle brackets will be duplicated. Markdown will use the URL as the link text *and* as the actual address. To show this, here is the HTML that Markdown will create:

```
<a href="https://daringfireball.net/projects/Markdown/">https://daringfireball.net/projects/Markdown/</a>
```

Email links can be created the same way:

```
<name@emailaddress.com>
```

This technique is certainly handy if we don't mind using a URL as link text, but what if we wanted to link to the same address, but use different text for the link?

Markdown supports two styles of links: *inline* and *reference*. In both styles, the text that is to be the link is set within square brackets and the URL where you want the link to point, in parentheses.

Inline Links

To create an inline link, we first, we type in our text, that will become the link, within square brackets followed immediately by the URL (the web address) in parenthesis:

```
[My site on the
Web](http://www.dyrobooks.com/)
```

The output will look like:

My site on the Web

We can add an optional title for the link, surrounded in quotes. Our link would then look like this:

```
[My site on the
Web](http://www.dyrobooks.com/ "book
preservation")
```

So far, we have used the link to be on a line by itself, but it doesn't have to be this way; we can use it within our text. The link is made exactly the same way, only it is within other text. This is known as *inline linking*. For example, let's say that I want to recommend a book inside of a paragraph. Again, the link is made the same way as above. The text that will be the link is placed within square brackets and the link itself placed within parentheses:

```
[Ashton's
Memorial](http://dyrobooks.com/collections/2
017/11/17/ashtons-memorial/)
```

We can insert this into a paragraph, like so:

```
It is believed, by some, that Daniel Defoe
was inspired to write *Robinson Crusoe*
after reading [Ashton's
Memorial](http://dyrobooks.com/collections/2
017/11/17/ashtons-memorial/), the true story
of Philip Ashton's capture by pirates, his
eventual escape, and living alone on Roatan
Island for 16 months before his rescue.
```

Here is what our output would look like:

It is believed, by some, that Daniel Defoe was inspired to write *Robinson Crusoe* after reading *Ashton's Memorial*, the true story of Philip Ashton's capture by pirates, his eventual escape, and living alone on Roatan Island for 16 months before his rescue.

The link is within the paragraph in a way that allows a reader to read the link as if it were a part of the text, making for a smoother reading experience. Clicking on the *Ashton's Memorial* link will send that user to the page that contains information about the book.

There may be times when you will want to keep inline links out of your text. Looking at the example, above, the URL does take up a good amount of space in our paragraph and it can make it difficult to find our place within the paragraph-- during an editing session--taking us out of the flow of writing because of the links. If we have several such links in a paragraph, it can become increasingly difficult to edit.

Generally, I do not mind having one inline link in a paragraph or a list. Any more than that, I use another linking method: *reference links*. Reference links allow you to move the markup-related metadata out of your sentences, and you can add URLs elsewhere without interrupting the flow of your writing.

Reference Links

Reference-style linking is a two-step process. First, we write our linking text, along with an id, within our paragraph. Next, we define that id, assigning it a URL, elsewhere in the document.

When we create a reference-style link within a paragraph, we use two sets of square brackets. The linking text is placed in one set of square brackets and the id (which can be any label we choose) into another set. For example, we have the following sentence in a paragraph:

```
This is an example of a link to
[dyrobooks][db] as a reference-style link.
```

If you wish, you can use a space to separate the sets of brackets:

```
This is an example of a link to [dyrobooks]
[db] as a reference-style link.
```

But where is the URL? That's the next step. We define our link label anywhere we want in the document, as long as it is on a line by itself, like so:

```
[db]: http://dyrobooks.com/ "Optional Title
Here"
```

Definitions are built like so:

- Square brackets containing the link identifier (optionally indented from the left margin using up to three spaces)
- followed by a colon
- followed by one or more spaces (or tabs)
- followed by the URL for the link
- optionally followed by a title for the link, enclosed in quotes or within parentheses

I usually put all of my definitions immediately underneath the paragraph or at the bottom of the page.

The following three link definitions are equivalent:

```
[db]: http://dyrobooks.com/ "Optional Title
Here"
[db]: http://dyrobooks.com/ 'Optional Title
Here'
```

```
[db]: http://dyrobooks.com/ (Optional Title
Here)
```

Note: There is a known bug in Markdown.pl 1.0.1 which prevents single quotes from being used to specify link titles. Some Markdown editors have fixed this, but others have not. I have left it here since it is in the Markdown documentation, but I recommend avoiding the use of single quotes.

Additionally, the link URL may be surrounded by angle brackets:

```
[db]: <http://dyrobooks.com/> "Optional
Title Here"
```

Lastly, you can put the title attribute on the next line and use extra spaces or tabs for padding. Longer URLs look better with this method:

```
[db]:
http://dyrobooks.com/collections/2017/11/17/
ashtons-memorial/
    "Optional Title Here"
```

Link definitions are only used for creating links during Markdown processing, and are stripped from the HTML output.

Link definition names may consist of letters, numbers, spaces, and punctuation--but they are *not* case sensitive. These two links, then, are equivalent:

```
[example link text][a]
[example link text][A]
```

We have covered several rules concerning the
structure of reference-style links. Ready for an
example? We will look at the actual markup and
then the output:

```
When it comes to sports, I can honestly
claim some mastery. I can put the ball
anywhere it isn't supposed to go. Passing a
[football][foot] to a receiver may be
difficult for me, but I can easily throw it
out of bounds. A [basketball][basket] will
never find the hoop when I shoot, but I can
easily hit a light fixture or the occasional
spectator. One can only imagine the damage I
can do with a [baseball][base].

[foot]:
https://en.wikipedia.org/wiki/American_footb
all
    "American Football"
[basket]:
https://en.wikipedia.org/wiki/Basketball
    "Basketball"
[base]:
https://en.wikipedia.org/wiki/Baseball
    "Baseball"
```

In this markup, my link text items are "football,"
"basketball," and "baseball." The id for these linked
text items are "foot," "base," and "basket."

Underneath the paragraph, I defined the identifiers
by adding a URL to a Wikipedia page about
football, basketball, and baseball. I also added the
optional link title (in quotes).

Now, our output when Markdown has processed it:

When it comes to sports, I can honestly claim some mastery. I can put the ball anywhere it isn't supposed to go. Passing a football to a receiver may be difficult for me, but I can easily throw it out of bounds. A basketball will never find the hoop when I shoot, but I can easily hit a light fixture or the occasional spectator. One can only imagine the damage I can do with a baseball.

Remember that the id definition grouping isn't displayed in our output. The grouping is used only to create the links. When Markdown processes the text, it removes the definition group, and we only see our paragraph with the working links.

Implicit Link Name Shortcut

There is a nifty shortcut that is worth a look: the *implicit link name* shortcut. This reference-style shortcut allows you to leave out the link identifier, in which case the link text itself is used as the identifier. Wc still use the second set of brackets, but left empty. For example, if we want to link the word "dyrobooks" to the dyrobooks.com web site, we only need write:

```
[dyrobooks][]
```

Elsewhere in the document, we define the link:

```
[dyrobooks]: http://www.dyrobooks.com/
```

Recall that link names can contain spaces, so this shortcut will work on link text that have multiple words:

```
In 1959, the US Postal Service attempted to
deliver mail via [cruise missile][],
successfully shipping 3,000 pieces of mail
from Virginia to Florida. It was the only
time a missile was used to carry mail in the
US.
```

Next, we define the link, like before, on a line by itself:

```
[cruise missile]:
https://postalmuseum.si.edu/collections/obje
ct-spotlight/regulus-mail.html
```

Our output will be:

In 1959, the US Postal Service attempted to deliver mail via cruise missile, successfully shipping 3,000 pieces of mail from Virginia to Florida. It was the only time a missile was used to carry mail in the US.

Images

The earliest documented account of anyone using diagrams in their texts was the pre-Socratic philosopher, Anaxagoras (c. 500 BCE – 428 BCE). Anaxagoras is sometimes regarded as an intellectual ancestor of the big bang theory, the first to theorize about the universe as ever expanding, and was also confident in the possibility of the existence of extra-terrestrials. He is also credited as being the creator of the school holiday.

I'm sure that Anaxagoras would have loved to have access to a computer with Markdown installed. It would have made his writing efforts more productive as well as easier. Fortunately, we do, and Markdown has some basic image support.

Remember that Markdown documents are plain text, so we don't see our images within the Markdown text because, just as with links, we reference (point to) an image, but we do see them in the output. The syntax for images resemble the syntax for links, allowing for two styles: *inline* and *reference*.

Inline Images

Inline image syntax looks like this:

```
![Alt text](/path/to/img.jpg)
```

or

```
![Alt text](/path/to/img.jpg "Optional
title")
```

That is:

- An exclamation mark: !
- followed by a set of square brackets, containing the `alt` attribute text for the image
- followed by a set of parentheses, containing the URL or path to the image, and an optional `title` attribute enclosed in double or single quotes

Let's look at a small example:

```
![my logo](path/to/logo.jpg)
```

Here, the word group in brackets: `my logo` is the linking text within a sentence that will also be the `alt` attribute. The path, in parentheses, points to the location of the image to be displayed.

Just as you can with links, you can include an optional title attribute for the image, like so:

```
![my logo](path/to/logo.jpg "This is my
logo")
```

Reference-Style Images

Reference-style image syntax looks like this:

```
![Alt text][id]

[id]: path/to/image.jpg
```

Where "id" is the name of a defined image reference. Image references are defined using syntax identical to link references but with the addition of the exclamation-mark before the first set of square brackets. Remember, just as with reference-style links, this is a two-step process.

The linking text is placed in one set of square brackets and the id (which can be any label we choose) into another set. For example, we have the following sentence in a paragraph. The word set, `my logo` is the text that will become the `alt` attribute and `logo`, in the second set of brackets, is the id:

```
This is an example of how to embed ![my
logo][logo] using reference-style image
syntax.
```

If you wish, you can use a space to separate the sets of brackets:

```
This is an example of how to embed ![my
logo] [logo] using reference-style image
syntax.
```

The next step is to define the link. We define our link label anywhere we want in the document, as long as it is on a line by itself, like so:

```
[logo]: http://path/to/logo.jpg
```

As with links, optional title attributes can be added to reference-style images too:

```
[logo]: http://path/to/logo.jpg  "Optional
Title Here"
```

Put together, our example looks like this:

```
This is an example of how to embed ![my
logo] [logo] using reference-style image
syntax.

[logo]: http://path/to/logo.jpg "Optional
Title Here"
```

Note: As of this writing, Markdown has no syntax for specifying the dimensions of an image; if this is important to you, you can use regular HTML `<img>` tags.

Ideally, you want to link to an image that is in your collection of files. It is bad manners to link to an image that is located on another domain. If you like an image on, say, Pixabay, copy that image and link to your copy--don't link to the one on Pixabay.

Horizontal Rules

Horizontal rules, lines that span the width of a page, are made by placing three or more hyphens, asterisks, or underscores on a line by themselves. You can put spaces between the asterisks or hyphens. Each of the following examples, below, will display a horizontal rule:

```
* * *

***

*****

- - -

----------------------------------------
```

Inline HTML

Markdown can handle many of the formatting tasks we ask of it, but it isn't a replacement for HTML. Markdown's syntax is very small, correlative to a Lilliputian subset of HTML tags. Markdown's syntax is a format for *writing* for the web. HTML is a *publishing* format. Markdown's formatting syntax is geared only to issues that can be conveyed in plain text. Markdown is not a replacement for HTML.

However, there may be a few times when a table in your document is a necessity. Basic Markdown doesn't support tables, but it does allow you to insert any HTML you wish.

This section is not intended to be an exhaustive treatment of HTML, but only to show that HTML can be used while providing an example or three. I am assuming that, if you insert HTML in your document, you know what you're doing.

For any markup that is not covered by Markdown's syntax, you simply use HTML itself. There's no need to preface it or delimit it to indicate that you're switching from Markdown to HTML; you just use the tags.

The only restrictions are that block-level HTML elements such as `<div>`, `<table>`, `<pre>`, `<p>`, etc.

must be separated from surrounding content by blank lines, and the start and end tags of the block should not be indented with tabs or spaces. Markdown is smart enough not to add extra (unwanted) `<p>` tags around HTML block-level tags.

For example, to add an HTML table to a Markdown article, make sure that there is at least one blank line between the paragraph and then create the table with HTML. When the table is made, add another blank line, like so:

```
This is a one line paragraph.

<table>
    <tr>
        <td>item in a table cell</td>
    </tr>
</table>

This is another one line paragraph.
```

Markdown formatting syntax is not processed within block-level HTML tags. In other words, you can't use Markdown-style `*emphasis*` within a code block of HTML. Any Markdown formatting, within a block of HTML, is ignored and treated literally. For example, a `<p>` element is a block-level tag. If we were to type:

```
<p>The Markdown *emphasis* marks, within the
HTML <p> tags, will not emphasize the text,
but will be displayed "straight-up." But if
you want to use emphasis within a paragraph,
just use the HTML tags for emphasis, such as
```

```
<em></em> and <strong></strong>. Markdown
formatting syntax does work within HTML
span-level tags, though.</p>
```

Span-level HTML tags such as **`<span>`**, **`<cite>`**, or
`<del>` can be used anywhere in a Markdown
paragraph, list item, or header. Unlike block-level
HTML tags, Markdown syntax works within span-
level tags. If you want, you can even use HTML
tags instead of Markdown formatting. If you would
rather use HTML **`<a>`** or **`<img>`** tags in your
document, instead of Markdown's link or image
syntax, you are free to use them. When I write, I use
all HTML tags in HTML code, keeping Markdown
syntax aside for the main text. Keeping the two
methods separate helps me keep things in order--
and the way I write my drafts, I need all the help I
can get.

Auto-Escaping of Special Characters

In HTML, there are a handful of characters that
require special treatment, such as **`<`**, **`>`**, and **`&`**. Left
angle brackets are used to start tags, right angle
brackets are used to end tags, and ampersands are
used to denote HTML entities. If you want to use
them as literal characters in HTML, you have to
escape them as entities, for example: **`<`**, **`>`**, and **`&`**.

Ampersands, and other characters, can be a pain
when writing HTML. If you want to write about

'AT&T', you need to write '`AT&amp;T`'. You even need to escape ampersands, as well as certain other characters within URLs. Here is a rather famous example. If you want to link to:

```
<!-- This is invalid --> <a
href="foo.cgi?chapter=1&section=2&copy=3&lan
g=en">...</a>
```

In this example, many browsers correctly convert `&copy=3` to ©=3, which may cause the link to fail. Since < is the HTML entity for the left-pointing angle bracket, some browsers also convert `&lang=en` to <=en. And one old browser even finds the entity §, converting `&section=` to §ion=2.

To fix these problems, you need to encode the URL as:

```
<!-- This is valid --> <a
href="foo.cgi?chapter=1&section=2&copy=3&lan
g=en">...</a>
```

in your anchor tag `href` attribute. This is easy to forget, and is probably the single most common source of HTML validation errors.

Fortunately, with Markdown we can use these characters naturally because Markdown takes care of all the necessary escaping for you. If you use an ampersand as part of an HTML entity, it remains unchanged; otherwise it will be translated into &.

So, if you want to include a copyright symbol in your article, you can write:

```
&copy;
```

and Markdown will leave it alone, seeing it as HTML, and displays the symbol. But if you write:

```
AT&T
```

Markdown will translate it to HTML so that the ampersand can be displayed in a web browser properly.

Similarly, if you use angle brackets as delimiters for HTML tags, Markdown will treat them as such. But if you write:

```
2 < 3
```

Markdown will translate it to:

```
2 < 3
```

However, inside Markdown code spans and blocks, angle brackets and ampersands are *always* encoded automatically. This makes it easy to use Markdown to write about HTML code. (As opposed to raw HTML, which is a terrible format for writing about HTML syntax, because every single < and & in your example code would need to be escaped.)

Conclusion

We have covered the ins-and-outs of basic Markdown and have seen that Markdown is an easy-to-use syntax for adding basic structure and formatting to your plain text documents. Even if you decided not to export your Markdown to HTML, it's very readable. In fact, as a student, I often write class notes, which will never be published, in Markdown--and if I do use some of those notes in a paper, much of that work is suitable as an advanced draft.

Basic Markdown, by itself, may not handle every single thing on a writer's wish list but it can do a huge portion of them. For more advanced tasks, there are numerous extensions "out there" that can take up the slack. If you decide to look into them, the things you've learned to do with basic Markdown will work with those extensions.

Whether your project is a web page, a paper, blog entry, article, or even a book, Markdown will certainly give a boost to your productivity.

Go forth and write--and may you meet with more success than you dare imagine.

Appendices

Here, you will find summary files: a cheat-sheet, a list of characters that can be escaped, a list of things to look for (a brief troubleshooting guide, of sorts) when your output isn't quite what you expect, and resources.

Lastly, for the musicians and music students, I added a short page on guitar tablature, which I discovered completely by accident. It turns out that Markdown's code block feature is perfect for it.

Markdown Cheat Sheet

There is a phrase that goes something like this: "*Read the instructions only as a last resort*." For those who absolutely will not read instructions, I provide this cheat sheet as familiarization with Markdown. For those who do read instructions, I present this cheat sheet as a refresher.

Markdown, a plain text markup format created by John Gruber. For more information and help, please visit his website at: http://www.daringfireball.net.

Markdown is a plain text *formatting* syntax. Punctuation characters are used to format the text. For example, an asterisk around a word or phrase gives it *emphasis*. Two asterisks around the word or phrase, make it **bold**.

Markdown, however, is more than an easy formatting scheme, it is also a software tool that converts the plain text formatting to HTML. Markdown is an appealing way to format plain text without having to resort to word processors, even if you don't have to convert to HTML.

Headings

```
# Level 1 Heading
## Level 2 Heading
### Level 3 Heading
#### Level 4 Heading
##### Level 5 Heading
```

```
###### Level 6 Heading

Level 1 Heading
===============

Level 2 Heading
---------------
```

Paragraphs

```
This is a paragraph. Paragraphs are ended
with a blank line.

This is a new paragraph.
```

Emphasis

You can do italics or even bold in two ways. The first is by surrounding the text with asterisks *, while the second is with underscores _.

```
This is *italics* with asterisks.
This is _italics_ with underscores.
This is **bold** with asterisks.
This is __bold__ with underscores.
```

Links

You can link to various websites:

```
Click [here](http://example.com "Optional
Title") to visit a website.
```

You can also use reference links:

```
[This][id] is a reference link which is
defined below.
```

```
[id]: http://example.com "Optional Title"
```

You can also use automatic links:

```
<http://automatic-link-to-url.com/>

<name@emailaddress.com>
```

Images

You can embed images like so:

```
![alternate text](./image.jpg "Optional
Title")
```

You can also use the same syntax as with reference links:

```
![alternate text][id] for a reference
defined below.

[id]: ./image.jpg "Optional Title"
```

Lists

You can use ordered lists:

```
1. Item one.
2. Item two.
3. Item three.
```

Or you can use unordered lists:

```
* Item one.
+ Item two.
- Item three.
```

You can mix and match with nested lists:

```
1. Item one.
   * Subitem one.
   * Subitem two.
2. Item two.
   - Subitem one.
   - Subitem two.
3. Item three.
   1. Subitem one.
```

Code Blocks

You can indent with four or more spaces or a tab character to create a code block:

```
This is a normal paragraph, followed by a
code block.

for (int i = 0; i < 10; i++) {
    System.out.println("i = " + i);
}

The above will be displayed as a
preformatted block of code.
```

Code Spans

You can surround a word with an accent grave (usually called a backtick) to show code. This is especially handy if we have some code (or some other word that we want to stand out) in the middle of a paragraph. For example, if we want to show "html," as well as the angle brackets, in a sentence, we can surround it with backticks:

```
This is how we can show `<html>` in a
sentence.
```

We will see:

This is how we can show **<html>** in a sentence.

You can use literal backticks by using more than
one backtick, such as with this example:

```
`` `escaped backtick` ``
```

Our output will be:

`escaped backtick`

Blockquotes

You can use email-style angle brackets to specify
block quotes, as follows:

```
> This is a block quote.

>> This is a nested (further indented) block
quote.
```

Horizontal Rules

Use three or more dashes -, underscores _, or
asterisks * for horizontal rules, like so:

```
---

***

___
```

You can even have spaces between each character:

    - - -

Backslash Escapes

When we use characters in Markdown to show formatting, these characters perform their function but the characters themselves aren't displayed in the output. When we surround a word with a single asterisk, the word is italicized:

```
*italic*
```

Our output will be:

italic

There are times, however, when we need to show the character. To do this, we 'escape' the character (some call this *suppression*). When we **escape** a character, we are using that character for a purpose other than which it was intended, and we do this by placing a backslash in front of the character.

```
\*italic\*
```

will display:

```
*italic*
```

Markdown allows you to use backslashes to escape special characters so that they can be shown as literal characters. For example, if you wanted to surround a word with literal asterisks, you can use a backslash before each asterisk, like so:

```
\*literal asterisks\*
```

The following special characters can be escaped
with a backslash:

```
\    backslash
`    accent grave (backtick)
*    asterisk
_    underscore
{}   curly braces
[]   square brackets
()   parentheses
#    hash mark
+    plus sign
-    minus sign (hyphen)
.    dot
!    exclamation mark
```

Gotchas and Watch-out-fors

Markdown is easy to use, but there are a few things to get used to. Line breaks, for example, aren't created as we would with say, a word processor. If your output isn't what you would expect, there could be a problem in your Markdown text. This section might be of help, without the need to search through the entire book.

If you need to force a line break in a paragraph, end the line with two spaces and hit the `<Enter>` key. Hitting `<Enter>` once, without the spaces, will not work. This is easy to forget. Your Markdown text may look right, but the output will be part of the paragraph as one block of text. If you want to see something like this haiku as your output:

An old pond!
A frog jumps in—
the sound of water.

but instead you see this:

An old pond! A frog jumps in— the sound of water.

add two spaces to the end of the first two lines in your Markdown text.

Markdown formatting syntax is ignored (displayed literally) in HTML block elements, but they are rendered in span elements.

If you start a sentence with a number and a period, backslash escape the period or else Markdown will treat it as a list element:

```
1879\. Einstein born during this year (March
14).
```

Markdown doesn't support list numbering (as of this writing) of items in an ordered list, but some Markdown editors have added support for it. Starting the list with "1" is highly recommended.

In atx-style headings, there should be a space between the last hash mark and the text. Not all Markdown editors require the space, but then again, some Markdown editors follow Markdown's rules more closely. Consider adding the space even if your Markdown editor doesn't require it:

```
Add the space between the last hash mark and
the following text, like so:

### Heading 3
```

There is a known bug in Markdown.pl 1.0.1 which prevents single quotes from being used to specify link titles. Some Markdown editors have fixed this, but others have not, so I recommend avoiding the use of single quotes:

```
[db]: http://dyrobooks.com/ 'Optional Title
Here'
```

Other Resources

Basic Markdown can do quite a bit and it can be easily integrated into your writing processes. Basic Markdown does have it limits, but there are extensions that can stretch its usefulness further. Some brief descriptions and links to some of these extended applications are presented here for the curious reader.

John Gruber's Markdown

http://daringfireball.net/projects/Markdown/

From the creator of Markdown - this is **the** resource when it comes to basic Markdown. I still refer to it.

CommonMark

http://commonmark.org

CommonMark is a solidly defined, highly compatible specification of Markdown. Since Markdown's release, several different implementations of Markdown have cropped up. Many have excellent extended features, but a document that renders one way on one system can render differently on another.

MultiMarkdown

http://fletcherpenney.net/multiMarkdown/

MMD is a superset of the Markdown syntax, originally created by John Gruber. It adds multiple syntax features (tables, footnotes, and citations, to name a few), in addition to the various output formats listed above (Markdown only creates HTML). Additionally, it builds in "smart" typography for various languages (proper left- and right-sided quotes, for example).

Pandoc

http://pandoc.org/

Pandoc is a universal document converter. If a document is written in Markdown, Word, reStructuredText, OpenOffice, HTML, LaTeX, and a host of other formats, Pandoc is a handy tool.

Pandoc especially shines with Markdown. It understands a number of useful Markdown syntax extensions, including document metadata (title, author, date); footnotes; tables; definition lists; superscript and subscript; strikeout; enhanced ordered lists (start number and numbering style are significant); running example lists; delimited code blocks with syntax highlighting; smart quotes, dashes, and ellipses; Markdown inside HTML blocks; and inline LaTeX. If strict Markdown compatibility is desired, all of these extensions can be turned off.

Github

https://help.github.com/articles/basic-writing-and-formatting-syntax/

GitHub is designed to help programmers. Markdown is used in creating documentation. If you're a programmer, or think you might be interested in using GitHub in the future, check this out. It has some interesting features.

Fountain

https://fountain.io/

I am no script writer, but I know a few people who are, which is the only reason I became aware of this one. Fountain allows you to write screenplays in any text editor on any device. Some editors have support for Fountain built in.

CriticMarkup

http://criticmarkup.com/

CriticMarkup is a tool of a different sort. It has no new features for document creation. Rather, it adds support for comments and marking text to add or remove. Some editors have already built in support for this.

Online Markdown Editors

There are several great Markdown editors for nearly every platform. Chances are, there will be a favorite that you will launch often. Not all editors work the same, and some have features that others do not, and it can take a good bit of time to find the one you like best. On the other hand, if you're on someone else's computer, they may not have a Markdown editor installed and you might not want to save your work on their machine. Likewise, a computer at work may be set up to where applications can't be installed. Perhaps you would rather not have extra software on your machine and would prefer to use an online tool. Not to worry–if a machine has access to the Internet, there are some good online Markdown editors. A few are listed here:

Dingus

https://daringfireball.net/projects/Markdown/dingus

First up is an online Markdown editor from the creator of Markdown, John Gruber. It's old and basic, but it works. I wonder if it is the first online Markdown editor; it could well be.

StackEdit

https://stackedit.io/

StackEdit is an in-browser Markdown editor that can sync your files with Google Drive, Dropbox and GitHub. It can also publish them as blog posts to Blogger, WordPress and Zendesk.

Ghost

https://ghost.org/

Ghost is a fully open source, hackable platform for building and running a modern online publication

Dillinger

https://dillinger.io/

Dillinger is a cloud-enabled, mobile-ready, offline-storage, AngularJS powered HTML5 Markdown editor.

TextDrop

https://www.textdropapp.com/home/Home

TextDrop is a web-based Markdown text editor that
enables you to access and edit text files in your
Dropbox folder. It was designed for situations
where you may not have Dropbox installed, such as
at work.

GitBook

https://www.gitbook.com/

GitBook is designed to help teams write, collaborate
and publish content online. It can get pricey to
subscribe, but if you create public and open source
material, there is no cost.

ASCII Guitar Tablature

Here is an unexpected use for Markdown that I found by accident. Markdown is good for ASCII guitar tabs. ASCII tab is a text file format used for writing guitar tablature (a form of musical notation) that uses plain ASCII numbers, letters and symbols.

Recently, I copied a sample arpeggio picking pattern and the only editor I had open at the time was a Markdown editor, so I copied it there. It worked perfectly. The tablature that I had copied is below:

```
e|--------2-----------------|
B|------3---3---------------|
G|----2-------2------------|
D|--0----------------------|
A|-------------------------|
E|-------------------------|
```

Indent each line as you would a code block. This will make the text a fixed width and the tab will be easier to read.

Basic Markdown may not be sufficient for complex pieces, but a music student may well find a way to effectively use Markdown for this.

Miscellaneous Notes

I have preserved a few documents in the past and the history of literature (and history in general) has always interested me. To share some of that interest, and to hopefully break up the monotony that can occur in a technical book, I have sprinkled some trivia here and there in both the main text and an example or two.

In no particular order, this section lists sources to those bits.

1866. First Known U.S. Train Robbery. Oct 6; Reno Gang.

https://www.history.com/this-day-in-history/first-u-s-train-robbery

NASA Apollo Spacecraft

Source:
https://www.nasa.gov/mission_pages/apollo/missions/index.html

Postal Service Cruise Missile

https://postalmuseum.si.edu/collections/object-spotlight/regulus-mail.html

---

Epictetus' Enchiridion

http://classics.mit.edu/Epictetus/epicench.html

Anaxagoras

Kenney, Anthony. Ancient Philosophy: A New History of Western Philosophy, Volume 1. Oxford University Press. New York. 2004. pp.24-26.

First Use of Bold Type

Twyman, Michael. "The Bold Idea: The Use of Bold-looking Types in the Nineteenth Century". Journal of the Printing Historical Society. 22 (107–143).

First Use of Italics

Hendrik D. L. Vervliet (2008). The
Palaeotypography of the French Renaissance:
Selected Papers on Sixteenth-century Typefaces.
BRILL. pp. 287–319.

History of the Hyperlink

http://www.newworldencyclopedia.org/entry/Hyper
link

Project Xanadu

http://www.xanadu.net/

The Code of Ur-Nammu

http://www.historyofinformation.com/expanded.php
?id=2241

The Code of Hammurabi

http://historyofinformation.com/expanded.php?id=2
240

Haiku Sample

https://www.poets.org/poetsorg/text/haiku-poetic-
form

About the Author

William Dyer is a continually caffeinated programmer/analyst who spends some of his spare time building e-books for a few of his writer friends, restoring old texts into digital form, and trying (key word there: 'trying') to play guitar. It was through restoration work that he caught the Markdown bug. He claims that he doesn't need a cure; he refuses to let go.

He isn't all that great on updating his sites (one still uses HTML from 1995), but his newest one is at:

http://www.dyrobooks.com/

He has to keep that one updated if he expects a good grade.